"don't" THINK OF
purple **spotted**
oranges

"don't" THINK OF

purple spotted

oranges

(The manual you were meant to get with your brain)

MARTIN
SHERVINGTON

New Millennium Books,
Vancouver

First published in Canada in 2001 by New Millennium Books
8036 Enterprise Street
Burnaby, British Columbia
V5A IV7 Canada
Tel: (604) 415-2444 Fax: (604) 415-3444

ISBN: 1-894067-32-0

Originated in Italy by Articolor
Printed and bound in Portugal by Printer Portuguesa

Project Editor Nic Kynaston
Art Editor Guy Callaby
Editor Sasha Hesletine
Editorial Assistants Ben Horslen, Emily Salter
Managing Art Editor Philip Gilderdale
Editorial Director Ellen Dupont
Art Director Dave Goodman
Editorial Coordinator Ros Highstead
Production Nikki Ingram
Illustrations by Martina Farrow/New Division
Photoshop montages by Guy Callaby

Picture credits
5 Andrew Sydenham; 6 PowerStock/Zefa; 7 Luiz Claudio
Marigo/Bruce Coleman; 10 Giles Chapman Library;
12 The Bridgeman Art Library; 14/15 Michael Keller/
The Stock Market; 25 Andrew Sydenham; 26/27 Gunter
Ziesler/Bruce Coleman; 28/29 Pictor International;
35 Jack Daniels/gettyone Stone, 39t Jane Burton/ Bruce
Coleman, 39b Frank Blackburn/Planet Earth Pictures;
40/41 Tim Davies/gettyone Stone; 44 Christer Fredricksson/
Bruce Coleman; 45l Hans Reinhard/Bruce Coleman;
45r Bruce Coleman; 52/53 (background) Bruce Coleman;
54/55 Corbis, 55 Randy Wells/ PowerStock/Zefa;
74 Images Colour Library; 77 Digital Vision; 78 Hans
Reinhard/Bruce Coleman; 82 Robert Harding Picture Library;
84/85 PowerStock/Zefa; 93/94 (skier) Robert Harding Picture
Library; 95 (deckchair) David Stoecklein/The Stock Market
The images on pages 24; 30; 35 (rose); 43; 56/57; 94; and 95
(hands) were specially taken by Paul Forrester

CONTENTS

1

Empower Yourself

2

Enhance Your Senses

3
Better Relationships

4
Reconnect Your Mind and Body

5
Enjoy Being Efficient and Well Organized

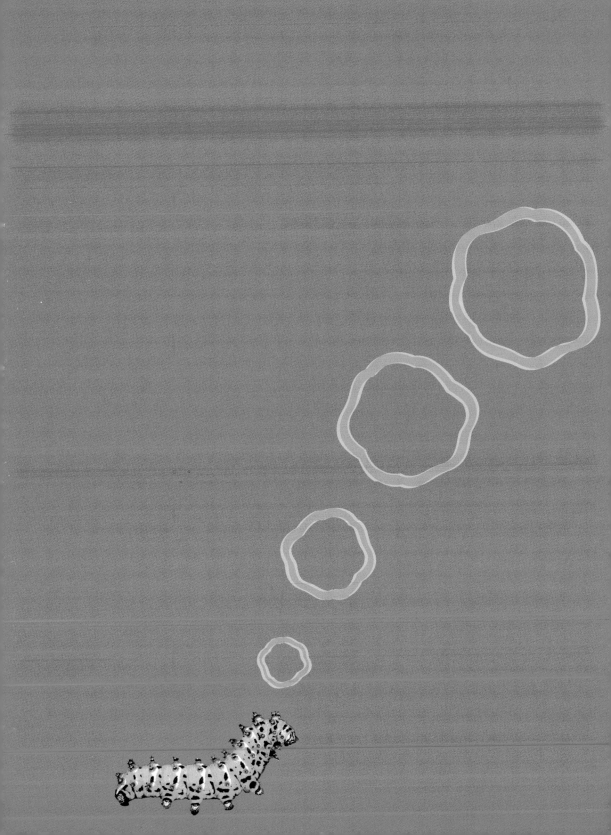

1

EMPOWER
YOURSELF

Have you noticed how many people lack confidence? Yes, we all have our bad times, but there are many simple and effective ways to turn these feelings around. In this chapter, learn how to revolutionize the way you feel about yourself and handle situations. No more morning blues or shaking knees at important moments. Instead, you will begin to build up a set of tools to improve the way you feel in any situation. You will discover how to improve your emotional state, so that you can alter the way you look at your world. Begin to take responsibility for empowering yourself and you will build up a set of tools to improve your life.

CHANGE THE WAY YOU TALK TO YOURSELF

We all have an inner voice in our heads. Sometimes it gives good advice, but more often it drags us down, knocking our confidence and self-esteem. But here is the GOOD news ...

Confident people have learned to use their internal voice to boost their positive emotions. They become their own greatest fans by paying themselves compliments coupled with daily pep talks.

So HOW do YOU do this?

Think of phrases you enjoy hearing.

Write them down and repeat them to yourself.

Whenever you need a boost, repeat them and see the effect they have on your mood.

I WILL ENJOY THIS DAY AS IT UNFOLDS

I am going to make a difference in my life

I DESERVE TO BE HAPPY

I have everything that I need at my fingertips

I FEEL GOOD ABOUT MYSELF

Life is great and I play a **POSITIVE PART** in it

I HAVE SO MUCH POTENTIAL and am willing to learn how to use it **MORE**

To add variety you can:

- **Talk FASTER to give yourself more motivation.**

- *Talk S-L-O-W-E-R when you want to relax.*

- **And if you want to feel sexy or funny, change your inner voice to suit your mood.**

PEOPLE ENJOY MY COMPANY

I want to be **KIND TO PEOPLE** that I know and respect.

I AM GOING TO DO WHAT IS IMPORTANT TO ME

I AM GOOD AT WHAT I DO

How to Put the Past Behind You

Do you find that you can't stop yourself from going over the low points of the day? Even though you know that dwelling on minor irritations and arguments spoils your mood, it's not easy to stop doing it. These memories often linger as depressing visual images, hanging over us like rain clouds.

You can put these bad thoughts behind you. By changing the way your brain stores these images, you will change the way you feel about the experience.

Maybe you had a flat tire that stopped your plans in their tracks. Bring up the memory of this event then notice what happens when you:

> *Move the image further away.*

> **Make it smaller.**

> *Turn it black and white.*

> **Place yourself in the memory rather than simply seeing it through your own eyes.**

These changes in perception distance you from the experience so that you can move on or forget about it altogether.

DO IT BETTER!

Do you ever find yourself making the same mistakes over and over? If so, instead of learning where you went wrong, you are repeating the same behavioural pattern time and again. Break this cycle by imagining you are performing the task better, and you'll find that you'll achieve much more.

Try the following five steps to prepare your brain for the achievements and success that lie ahead ...

1 *Visualize a situation that you want to improve.*

2 *Imagine yourself acting differently in this situation and see your performance improving in your mind's eye.*

3 *Watch the action unfold as in a video. How do you feel? How do the other people in your mental video react to what's going on?*

4 *Play the scene in different ways until you are satisfied with the results you are visualizing.*

5 *Think of a sign to help you activate this new behaviour in real life. For example, it could be seeing a goal post, hearing somebody's voice or walking into a room.*

By asking yourself "What could I have done differently?" after an event, you can use this method to improve your results time after time. You can now edit the past and use your "inner video" to guide you towards success.

GIVE IT UP
FOR GOOD!

We all have **BAD HABITS** that we want to give up, from **SMOKING** or **DRINKING TOO MUCH** to **NAIL BITING** or **OVER-EATING**.

But it's hard to give up something you enjoy. Like many people, if you focus on the negative aspects of your bad habit, such as the damage to your health, you might think it is easier to give up. Even then, despite knowing the harm you're doing to yourself, giving up the bad habit can be a struggle.

You can often boost your willpower if you give yourself a new goal when you give something up. Replacing the benefits of your bad habit with new benefits and rewards makes it easier to kick the habit.

Follow these four stages to give up your bad habits for good:

STAGE 1 *Ask yourself "What benefit do I get from this habit?"*

STAGE 2 *Then ask "How else can I achieve the same benefit? Is there any reward for giving up my bad habit? For instance, "If I stopped eating chocolate, would I lose weight and feel fitter?"*

STAGE 3 *Next ask "Would I give up my bad habit if I could have this new reward instead?" That way you will know if you are just fooling yourself about wanting to give it up.*

STAGE 4 *Finally, set a goal and promise yourself a new reward such as "If I stop biting my nails for three days, I will buy myself a new shirt". Set longer-term goals with rewards until you have well and truly broken your old habits.*

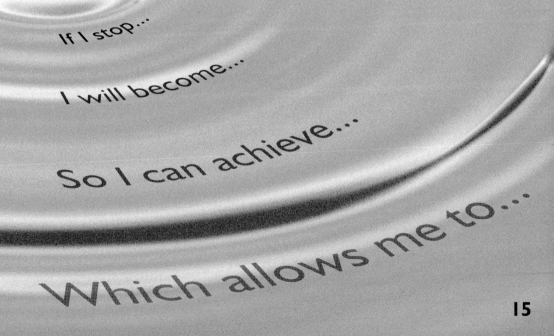

If I stop…

I will become…

So I can achieve…

Which allows me to…

Tune in to the Right EMOTION

Could a quick *CLICK OF THE HEELS* really whisk you away to Kansas? Maybe not, but it could certainly help you towards a better emotional state.

Remember how a song from many summers ago can bring back the same feeling as when you heard it the first time?
Or a friendly touch on the shoulder helped a friend feel good.

If you have positive feelings about something or someone, you can turn them into triggers to access positive emotions at will. Whether it's clicking your heels, pressing a thumb and finger together or any other gesture or movement, you will be able to instantly recreate the feeling like flicking on a switch.

There are many times when you can try this out:

When you want more confidence

When you want to feel sexier

When you need to relax

1 *Choose an emotion that you would like to access at will, such as contentment or enjoyment.*

2 **Pick a visual symbol to represent this emotion. It could be a favourite pair of shoes or an adored pet.**

3 *Choose a word or phrase to say to yourself – "Yippee!!" or "Hooray" perhaps – when you visualize your symbol.*

4 **Alter your posture to reflect a positive state of mind. Repeat the process of changing your posture five times.**

5 *Pick a physical anchor, for example, clicking your heels together like Dorothy or pressing your ear lobe.*

6 **Then "click those heels" to fire up that emotion. Hey presto!**

Swish
Patterns

Have you ever put off *FILLING IN FORMS*, *CLEANING THE HOUSE* or even *EXERCISING* because you can't face doing it? Imagine how happy you'd be if you felt positive about annoying tasks. You could then tackle them with enthusiasm instead of constantly putting them off until later.

> *SWISH PATTERNS will help you learn*
> *to love the tasks you used to hate.*

Use the swish-pattern technique when you want to change a *NEGATIVE* emotion to a *POSITIVE* one. Once you've mastered swish patterns, you'll be proud of what you've completed, not filled with guilt about chores left undone.

1 Visualize a *DREADED TASK* that you want to view more *POSITIVELY*, such as filling in your tax return.

2 Then think of an image of yourself feeling *GOOD* and *POSITIVE* about completing the tax form.

3 Imagine this *SECOND* image in a small box at either of the bottom corners of your *FIRST* image.

4 Now **SWISH** the images. Do this by quickly **REPLACING** the first image with the second.

5 Repeat this process **20** times.

In future, whenever you think of the DREADED TASK, your brain will SWISH to the up-beat image, making you feel POSITIVE about what you have to do.

PROGRAMMED FOR SUCCESS

BANISH the word

"TRY"

from your vocabulary!

TRY

TO TOUCH THE CENTRE OF THIS TARGET

No doubt you have touched the centre of the target – but this is touching the target, not trying to touch it. Now **TRY** to touch it again. If you touch it, you have not **TRIED** to try hard enough.

Usually we don't think of "trying" as a state of not achieving. We often "try" to get things done and then wonder why we don't achieve them. By removing this word from your vocabulary, you become a DOER, not a trier. You can then say you're DOING something, or are in the process of doing it, which then tells your brain that you are being pro-active and succeeding in what you are doing.

WONDERFUL YOU!

There are many things that other people see as your unique qualities. But YOU might not realize what they are.

You have UNIQUE qualities

Complete the following exercises to remind yourself of those unique qualities:

1 Find a piece of paper and write down some of your unique good points. To find your POSITIVE SIDE, think of positive comments that other people make about you. You don't even have to believe them yourself! List between five and eight qualities.

2 Recall an image of yourself. If you feel a bit down, this might well be a small dark image. Imagine your friends noticing and commenting on your GOOD POINTS, and see yourself accepting their compliments gracefully rather than shrugging them off.

helpful sympathetic friendly easy-going compassionate

GENEROUS CARING WARM WITTY TRUSTING

tender gentle wise funny clever honest

The image will begin to change. It may:

Increase in size.

Move closer to you.

Become brighter and more colourful.

You can even step into the image to make it more real.

3 When you are feeling low and your self-esteem withers, CONJURE UP this image and let yourself focus on your unique qualities.

4 You will find that what you've IMAGINED starts HAPPENING more and more because you are beginning to adopt that positive image in real life as well as in your mind's eye.

AVOID
DON'T

As you are reading this, **DON'T** think of freshly squeezed orange juice ... and definitely **DON'T** think about **PURPLE SPOTTED ORANGES**.

FIND YOURSELF THINKING OF

ORANGES?

That just proves

the power of

"DON'T" – it

makes you think

the OPPOSITE

of what you should

be thinking.

The same principle applies to worries. It is far more effective to say **"Things usually work out fine"** than the normal **"Don't worry"**.

Focus on what you WANT in life, not what you DON'T want.

Come up with an "I WANT" statement that will make you feel more active and full of positive energy.

Now you can truly understand the power of

"DON'T"

2
ENHANCE YOUR SENSES

How do you view the world? It will certainly have changed since you were a child when a summer day seemed to last forever. Your awareness of the world is filtered through your senses first, so what you see, hear, feel, taste and smell has a huge impact on your life and your world-view. In this chapter, learn to open your senses to new experiences and be more attuned to the richness that is on offer to you. No matter how much enjoyment you already get from life, these tools will give you more.

VISUAL

TUNING

One of the senses we use most is the *VISUAL* one. From advertising to television, we are constantly bombarded by thousands of colours and shapes.

But do you ever think about *choosing* what you see?

Follow these exercises to regain a sense of fun and excitement in what you see. Look at the world in a totally different way and train your eyes to change the way in which your mind works.

Spend a week noticing just ONE COLOUR *Train yourself over a week to "filter" for the colour red. Look at a field of poppies and see beyond the mass of green with dots of colour, consciously picking out the red. Every time you see the colour red, make a mental note.*

Attempt to get back a child-like sense of WONDER

Imagine you've never seen an elevator before. What a concept – walls open up and people walk into them! What on earth is that all about? As adults we often forget how bizarre the world around us appears to young children.

Imagine what a building would look like if YOU were able to design it yourself

What colour would the building be? Would you design a purple glass building and crown it with a tall spiralling roof-garden? Draw a mixture of the building of your imagination and what you see around you. The result might not be great art, but it will certainly help you look at things in a fresh way.

TASTE IT!

Does your mind wander when you do something habitual like eating a meal? Do you think "Right, after this I'm going to ..."? Do you sometimes forget that you have eaten at all? You are missing out on the experience of eating AND the flavour of your food.

Sample a favourite food and for once REALLY savour the taste. It doesn't matter if it is chocolate, fruit or a flavourful snack.

Imagine this is the first time you have eaten your favourite food. What does it really taste like? How does it make you feel? Spend a couple of minutes slowly chewing each mouthful – where in your mouth do you feel the pleasurable sensations?

Take time to REALLY appreciate your food

Remember the enjoyment you had in really tasting what you ate. In future, eat more slowly and concentrate on really tasting the flavours. You will gain more satisfaction from meal times.

FEEL IT!

Every day, even on average ones, you are riding a *ROLLER COASTER* of emotions.

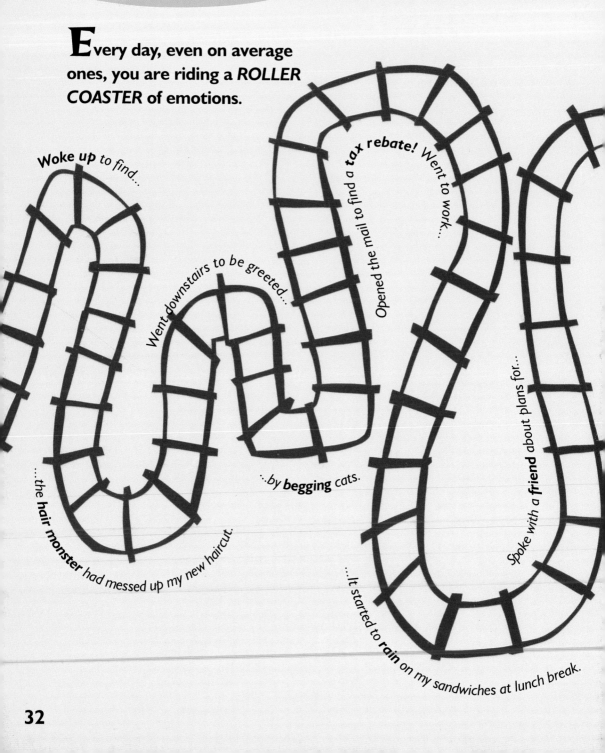

Woke up to find...

...the **hair monster** had messed up my new haircut.

Went downstairs to be greeted...

...by **begging** cats.

Opened the mail to find a **tax** rebate! Went to work...

Spoke with a **friend** about plans for...

...It started to **rain** on my sandwiches at lunch break.

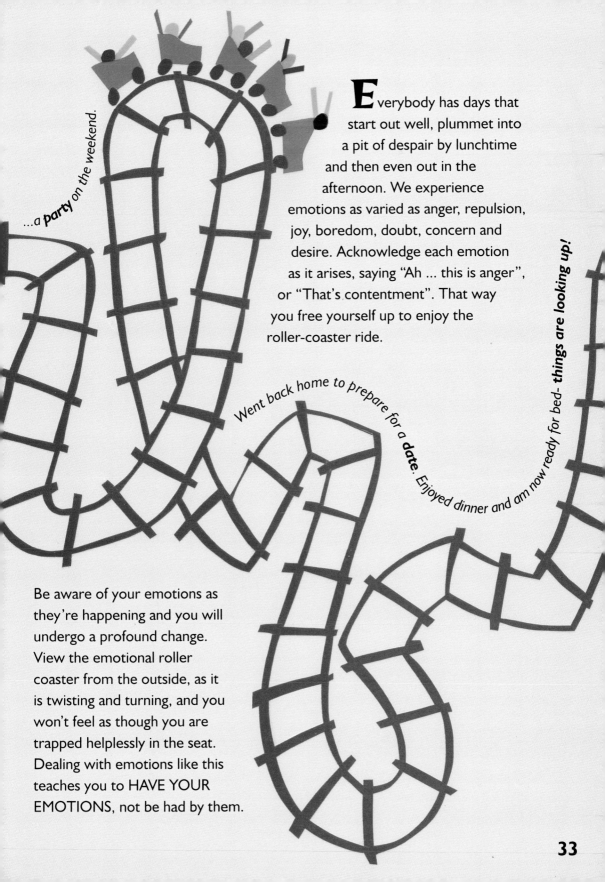

...*a party* on the weekend.

Everybody has days that start out well, plummet into a pit of despair by lunchtime and then even out in the afternoon. We experience emotions as varied as anger, repulsion, joy, boredom, doubt, concern and desire. Acknowledge each emotion as it arises, saying "Ah ... this is anger", or "That's contentment". That way you free yourself up to enjoy the roller-coaster ride.

Went back home to prepare for a *date*. Enjoyed dinner and am now ready for bed- *things are looking up!*

Be aware of your emotions as they're happening and you will undergo a profound change. View the emotional roller coaster from the outside, as it is twisting and turning, and you won't feel as though you are trapped helplessly in the seat. Dealing with emotions like this teaches you to HAVE YOUR EMOTIONS, not be had by them.

33

SMELL THE ROSES

We are exposed to hundreds of smells every day. Some of these we breathe in as if we could eat them. Other times we hold our noses.

Does the smell of coffee wake you up in the morning? Or does the scent of a perfume you like make you notice how attractive the person wearing it is? But what about the dog that looks cute but smells a bit off?

Pick two different places such as the garden and the kitchen. What smells, good and bad, do you notice? Do you see how often you avoid the smells you don't like instead of accepting them as and when they arise?

If you train your senses to be numb every time you smell a nasty odour, you are in danger of becoming numb to great smells as well.

Life consists of things we call pleasant and others we call unpleasant.

Learn to accept what arises in your senses as it happens and you will keep yourself on an even keel emotionally.

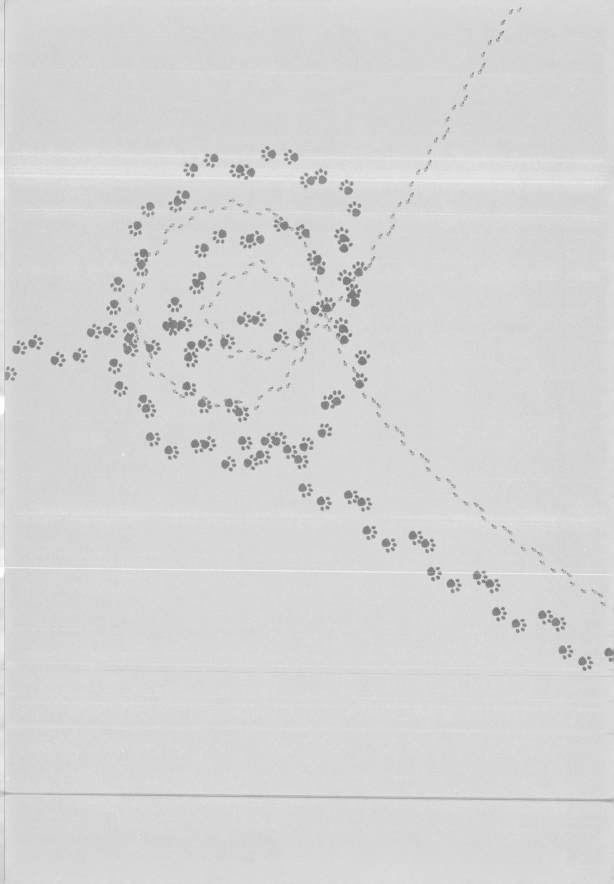

3
BETTER
RELATIONSHIPS

Do you assume that your way of doing things and thinking is always right? In the unlikely case of this being true, you can't expect everybody else to agree with you. In this chapter, step outside your own world for once to see what is important to other people. A lot of the time the key to better relationships is seeing the other guy's point of view. These simple techniques will help you to improve your relationships on all levels.

EYE CUES

Have you noticed that people move their eyes when they are thinking of an answer to a question? These eye movements are not random. When people search mentally for information, they reveal how they are thinking, as outlined below:

UPWARDS: visually accessing images
ACROSS: remembering or making up sounds
DOWN: experiencing feelings and talking to themselves

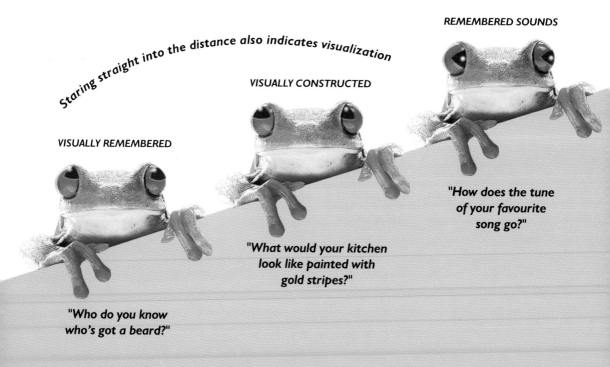

Staring straight into the distance also indicates visualization

REMEMBERED SOUNDS

VISUALLY CONSTRUCTED

VISUALLY REMEMBERED

"How does the tune of your favourite song go?"

"What would your kitchen look like painted with gold stripes?"

"Who do you know who's got a beard?"

People tend to look to the left to remember something, and to the right to construct, see or hear the future. If you pose a question, about 90% of people will follow these patterns with their eyes while searching for information.

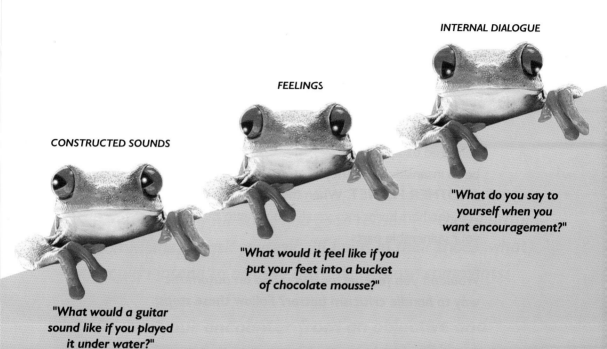

CONSTRUCTED SOUNDS

"What would a guitar sound like if you played it under water?"

FEELINGS

"What would it feel like if you put your feet into a bucket of chocolate mousse?"

INTERNAL DIALOGUE

"What do you say to yourself when you want encouragement?"

Next time you have a conversation with someone, ask questions like, "**What did you do last weekend?**", or "**Have you got plans for a holiday next year?**" Look at the way their eyes move as they reply and match your response to theirs. Do this by talking to them in the way they are thinking. For example, if someone is accessing visual information, make comments like: "**I see what you mean**", or "**That seems like a bright idea**". If someone is accessing sounds, say: "**I hear what you're saying**", or "**Sounds good**". With someone accessing feelings, try: "**That must have felt great**", or "**I know you'll love it**". You will notice an immediate positive response; people will feel more at ease with you because you have made the effort to communicate in the way that works best for them.

REMEMBER NAMES FIRST TIME!

How many times have you forgotten someone's name ten seconds after being introduced to them? You are not alone. The lucky few who ARE good at remembering names make them fun to remember, turning the process into a game.

By associating a name, for example, Steve Keates, with "size-ten feet", you are using both a visual cue – Steve with feet – and an aural cue – the rhyme – so it's easy to remember his name first time. Likewise with Mr "bushy tail" Fox, Mr "king of the jungle" Lyons and Mrs Cowles-rhymes-with Owls.

"More tea, thingummy?"

When you are introduced to someone, look at their features and what they are wearing so you have a visual cue to associate with their name.

You don't have to make your link rhyme with a name, but it can make things easier.

EASE MEGA-PROBLEMS WITH METAPHORS!

When things go wrong, we so often say things like "It has all fallen apart" and "Life is in ruins". Whereas when they go well we tend to say, "I feel over the moon" and "Life is like a bowl of cherries". The metaphors we use for life will often govern our interaction with it.

When you begin to relate more with your personal metaphors, you can allow them to transform the way you view the world. You will also be able to aid others to see situations differently. So is it possible for us to change the metaphors that we use?

Imagine that you have a friend who is very busy and getting worn out. If you ask them to describe what they are feeling, they might say, "I feel like I am carrying the weight of the world". If they haven't used a metaphor, you can ask them to describe their problem in that way. You then ask them a series of questions to bring the metaphor to life.

Ask these questions...

Where is this weight?

Does it have a colour or a shape?

Where did it come from?

What happens just before it comes back again?

What does it do to you?

What was it before it became a weight?

What is happening to it now?

Metaphors often transform themselves as you work out new ways of looking at them. As the metaphor unfolds, your friend's perspective of the problem will change and their ability to deal with it improve. Put simply, bringing your metaphor to life changes your perception of the problem, often in a positive way.

LEARN TO TURN BURDENS INTO A FORCE THAT CAN ACTUALLY LIFT YOU UP AND LET YOU FLY!

KEY INTO OTHER PEOPLE'S MIND-SETS

Have you noticed that certain patterns in your personality make your behaviour predictable? Using your own standard patterns of thinking is a bit like seeing the world through a pair of tinted glasses. If you need to make a decision, it will always be assessed through the same colour lenses – in other words, by always using the same criteria.

SOME STANDARD THINKING PATTERNS ARE:

TOWARDS / AWAY FROM *Some people motivate themselves to work towards goals while others move away from what they don't want to happen.*

SELF / OTHER *Individuals either make decisions according to their own opinions or through seeking the external help of others.*

OPTIONS / PROCEDURES *Some people play with different approaches to a problem while others tend to follow specific tried and tested procedures.*

BIG PICTURE / DETAILS

Some people enjoy working on the big picture while others are happier looking at the minute detail.

PRO-ACTIVE / REACTIVE

Pro-active people initiate action while reactive people are motivated into action by external events.

SIMILARITY / DIFFERENCE

Some people see what is similar when they make a comparison, while others notice differences.

By listening to what people say, you can work out their basic thought patterns and tailor your response to that. If someone says, "I will get down to the nitty-gritty of work so I can have a holiday", you can identify them as detail-conscious and motivated towards a specific goal.

Use this knowledge to your advantage. For example, a colleague who loves detail may NEVER see the big picture, but their love of detail can be a positive attribute in many situations.

Getting on the Right Level

Do you know how much your use of language reveals about your attitude to life? If you learn to interpret language on the series of ascending levels shown below, you'll be able to interact with people more succinctly and help others to solve their problems.

THE LEVELS ARE:

1 ENVIRONMENT – *refers to our surroundings and other people*

2 BEHAVIOUR – *covers the actions we take*

3 CAPABILITY – *considers our skills*

4 BELIEF – *examines our innate beliefs*

5 IDENTITY – *questions our own sense of self*

6 SPIRITUAL – *identifies our individual ultimate purposes in life*

Take a simple problem like recycling. Perhaps someone doesn't recycle their paper at work. To change this situation, ask them why they don't recycle and interpret their answer by looking at the level their comments stem from.

Are they being stopped in their attempts to recycle by:
– a lack of recycling bins? (ENVIRONMENT – easily changed)
– a belief that recycling is not worthwhile? (BELIEF – may require discussion)
– a perception that they are not a person who recycles? (IDENTITY – will require a change in the way they see themselves)

Analyze the response to see which level it lies on and address the situation.

Changes made on a lower level tend to have little effect on higher ones, but if you change your profound spiritual beliefs, a change often occurs at the environment level. For instance, by deciding that recycling is a moral responsibility (SPIRITUAL), you become the sort of person who recycles. "Top down" change can have a deep and lasting effect on the way you live.

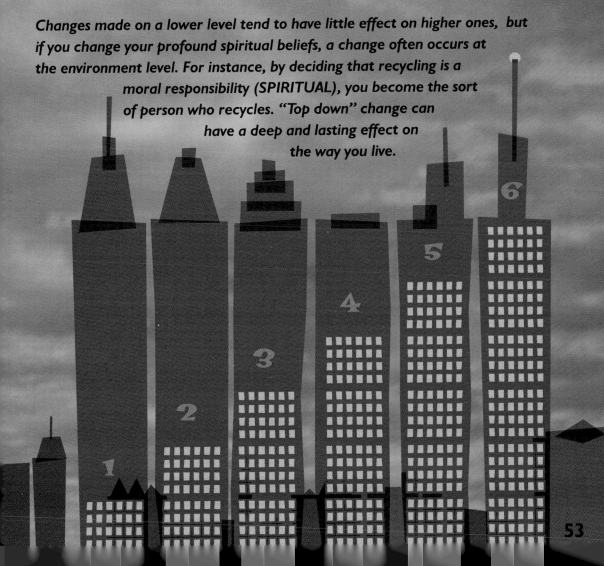

MIRRORING
IMAGES

Do you enjoy "people watching"? Most of us do. Look around you and notice how people who are comfortable with each other automatically mirror each other's body language – sitting in the same position, folding their arms or crossing their legs in the same way. When people are not relaxed with each other, their postures often don't match.

If you spend some time monitoring somebody's body language, you'll learn a lot about their emotional state. Going one step further and "matching" their body language will increase the empathy between you, which has enormous benefits in both social and work situations.

Watch your subjects from their heads downwards. Notice the way their bodies move and try to imagine how you would feel if you were doing the same thing. If someone is very elated, raise your level of animation to increase your rapport with them.

Listen to people's voices. If someone is speaking very quietly, lower your voice to emulate theirs. If someone is loud, be loud yourself. Put your own feelings to one side for a while and devote your attention to deciphering somebody's state of mind. As long as you are relaxed and confident in what you are doing, no-one will pick up on your conscious efforts to copy them.

With practice, you'll soon be able to use this method without thinking and as a result you'll have another subtle means of putting your point of view across to people. You'll have the tools to fit into any situation, no matter how unusual. You're a social chameleon in the making!

LEARN TO BE

SPECIFIC

Do you make small problems seem bigger? On a bad day, do you moan that life is tough? That's being negative – and it's not true anyway! It's just one bad day, not your whole life! It's probably one single tough moment in the day which leaves a nasty taste in your mouth. When you understand what is really making you feel bad, you can start being more objective.

Ask yourself questions to get to the specifics of a problem and it becomes manageable because it is reduced to a realistic size.

"Is it really all of your life?"
"No, but my work is hard."

"Which part of your life is tough?"
"All of my life is tough."

"Which part of work is hard?"
"Meetings are very hard."

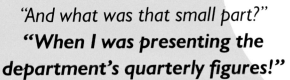

"And what was that small part?"
**"When I was presenting the
department's quarterly figures!"**

"During the
whole meeting?"
**"No, just a small
part, really."**

"When don't they
listen to you ?"
**"During the
meeting today."**

"How are
they hard?"
**"People just don't
listen to me."**

*This process of questioning experiences
and emotions to get to the specifics of
a situation will show you that mountains
are often really only molehills.*

REFRAMING: A STORY YOU CAN LEARN FROM

Do you find yourself cursing every time things go wrong? Turn round the way you view difficult situations to see life as it is – one great big experience!

There is a story that illustrates this well:

An old daoist farmer had a son, who broke his leg. The villagers said, **"That's terrible!"** but the farmer said, **"It's neither good nor bad"**.

Next day the army came and took all the boys in the village – except the farmer's son who had a broken leg. The villagers said, **"That's great!"** but the farmer said, **"It's neither good nor bad"**.

The next day, the old man's horse ran away, and the villagers said, **"That's terrible!"** but the farmer said, **"It's neither good nor bad"**.

A couple of days later the horse returned, in foal, with a stallion. And the villagers said ...

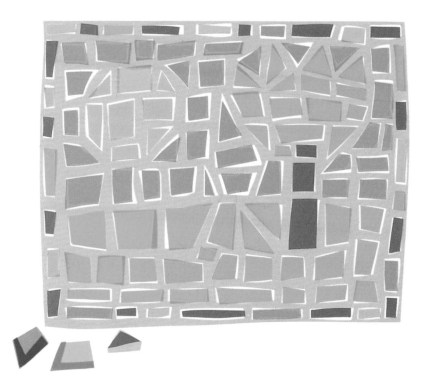

Get the point? Apply that premise to your own life. You rush to a meeting, arriving hassled, to find that the others are late as well. When you understand that life tends to fall into balance over time, it's easier to accept whatever happens to you.

Next time a vase falls from the shelf, say **"Hey, it's time to learn how to make a mosaic!"** Turn every experience into a positive and learning one instead of a negative and hurtful one. Life will instantly become a better place.

Help turn around other people's days, too. When somebody claims that loosing a business deal has ruined their plans, respond with **"Maybe it's given you time to make an even bigger deal"**. Use the same positive approach if someone is turned down for a date. If they are down, counter with, **"No, it's fantastic, you can go out clubbing and meet someone new!!!"**

4

RECONNECT YOUR MIND AND BODY

Do you regard your mind and body as part of the same whole?
Or as two distinct entities that have nothing to do with each other?
Too often your body ends up as a second-rate carriage for your mind.
In this chapter, learn the tools to redress that balance.
Remake the connection between your mind and body to be
energized and empowered. You'll feel like a whole person
again and be able to tackle much more in life.

LEARN TO LOVE
YOUR LEAST
FAVOURITE
BODY PART

Is there a bit of your body that you actively dislike? For instance, lots of people think that their legs are not long enough, while others resent internal organs which have let them down and made them ill. A common way of dealing with this is to detach from the offending body parts and turn them into enemies. By learning to accept them, however, you'll find a greater peace of mind.

TAKE TIME OUT TO PRACTISE THIS EXERCISE:

Lie down on the floor and relax.

Feel your body in contact with the floor.

Explore your body with your mind, feeling it from the tips of your toes to the top of your head. Picture your insides as well, and send positive thoughts to every area of your body.

Approach your least favourite body part and for once take the time to give it special attention. Acknowledge it, accept it and learn to love it instead of ignoring it.

Imagine tender kisses touching that body part, whether it is external or internal. Feel that area being covered in love.

Smile as you start to feel reconnected to your whole body.

FINDING INNER PEACE IN THREE EASY STEPS

Do you ever *SLUMP* in a chair at the end of the day, feeling worn out? Here are some simple remedies:

1 *CHANGE YOUR POSTURE*: Sit up straight, square your shoulders and be positive. People who feel positive about life reflect this in the way they hold themselves.

Next time your lower back caves in, move into an *UPRIGHT* position. It's difficult to feel miserable if you sit up straight. If you unwittingly revert to slouching, sit up straight again as soon as you notice.

2 *CHECK YOUR BREATHING*: Do you breathe from your abdomen like small children do? Or from high up in your chest? If you do breathe shallowly, expand your lower chest as you breathe in and pull it in gently as you breathe out. Get used to breathing from the abdomen again and you'll be more relaxed and energetic.

3 LEARN TO MEDITATE: Take charge of your mind by learning to focus. Sit somewhere quiet, and concentrate on your thoughts. Feel your breath entering and leaving your body for a minute or so and your thoughts will start to dissolve, leaving your mind clear. Focus on drawing breath through your nostrils for added concentration.

Does your mind wander? Simply re-focus your attention on your breathing.

USE YOUR WHOLE BRAIN!

Are there times when someone's name is on the tip of your tongue, but you can't quite get to it? And the minute you stop wrestling with it, the name pops to the front of your brain!

Where ARE these thoughts stored? How can you tap into this?

Your conscious mind is just the tip of an iceberg – your unconscious mind is much, much bigger. It stores all your life's information and oversees the functioning of your body. Tapping into this vast source of knowledge will enhance your abilities one-hundred fold.

Encourage your unconscious mind to work for you by using the following technique:

1 Ask your unconscious mind if it is willing to communicate with you. Ask for a signal if the answer is "yes". This will often take a physical form, such as a tingle or a subtle quickening of the heart.

2 Ask for the signal to be repeated so you know when it's the real thing.

3 Direct a question to your unconscious. Do you feel a repeat of the signal? If so, the answer to your question is a positive one. No signal? The answer is a "No".

COMMUNICATE with your UNCONSCIOUS

– When you need encouragement to make a decision

– When you need to access information you once knew

– When you need an insight into your personal needs

HOW TO USE BOTH SIDES OF YOUR BRAIN!

Did you know that you spend more time using one side of your body than the other? Unless you are completely ambidextrous, one side is always used predominantly, be it for writing, painting or playing sports.

WHICH SIDE DO YOU FAVOUR?

A connection exists between the side of your body that you favour and your brain. The left side of your brain relates to the right side of your body, and vice versa. Learn to balance the use of your body to enhance your ability.

EACH SIDE of your brain has a DIFFERENT focus:

LEFT SIDE: rational, attends to detail, analytical, makes lists, sequential.

RIGHT SIDE: intuitive, sees big picture, creative, recognizes colour and dimension, imaginative.

A work-out for your brain:

Pick up a pen and start to doodle with the hand you
don't normally use. At first you'll find it difficult to
judge distance and you'll have to concentrate to
move the pen. Keep doodling and let your mind
drift off. It should become easier after a while.

Begin to doodle.

When you are on the phone,
let your "wrong" hand scribble
away and look at your
doodle when you've finished
the call. What sort of shapes have
you made? What do they look like?

**Other pastimes, such as juggling or T'ai chi, can also redress
the balance of your body. Although they take a while to
master, your brain will quickly open up new connections
and pathways to make the learning process easier.**

GET IN TOUCH WITH YOUR DREAM LIFE

Have you ever experienced a dream that was so real you thought you were awake? Did you wake up and think, "Wow!"? This phenomenon, called lucid dreaming, occurs when you are fast asleep and then become aware that the experience you are having is really a dream.

You can train yourself not only to remember your dreams but also to wake up within the confines of a dream, explore your surroundings and begin to change what is happening there. One technique is to train yourself to look at your hands in a dream and treat this as the signal to direct the action.

If you can't usually recall your dreams, making a mental note to be more aware of them just before you drop off to sleep will help.

You'll discover a whole new life just a few snores away and will soon find that you can even change the course of your dreams.

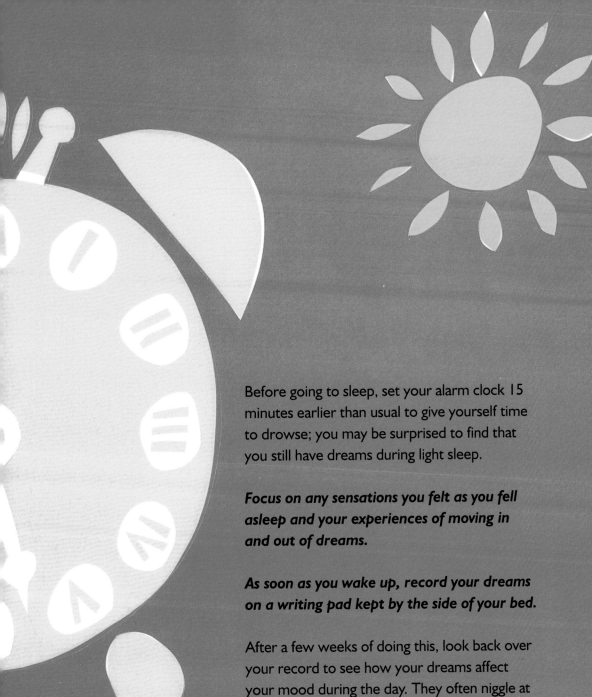

Before going to sleep, set your alarm clock 15 minutes earlier than usual to give yourself time to drowse; you may be surprised to find that you still have dreams during light sleep.

Focus on any sensations you felt as you fell asleep and your experiences of moving in and out of dreams.

As soon as you wake up, record your dreams on a writing pad kept by the side of your bed.

After a few weeks of doing this, look back over your record to see how your dreams affect your mood during the day. They often niggle at the back of your mind; if you understand that this is natural, you will not be troubled by them.

5

ENJOY BEING EFFICIENT AND WELL ORGANIZED

Does your home sometimes feel like a structured world one day and the next an alien place of chaos and disaster? Does this apply to other areas of your life as well as your personal space? Would you like to be efficient and well-organized? Well, you're in luck — read this chapter to discover unplumbed depths of enthusiasm that you didn't know you had. Take advantage of a few simple tools to improve your effectiveness by one hundred per cent. Spend your life living, not dithering!

ORGANIZE THE CHAOS IN YOUR LIFE

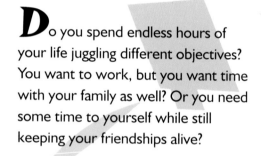

Do you spend endless hours of your life juggling different objectives? You want to work, but you want time with your family as well? Or you need some time to yourself while still keeping your friendships alive?

When you're faced with a clash of priorities like these, it's time for action. By finding the answers to the following questions, clashing priorities, or indeed any other problem, will soon become manageable again.

After all, a problem is just something that you wish was SOMETHING ELSE.

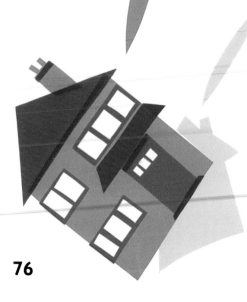

What do I want instead?

Don't think of purple spotted oranges! For example, "I don't want to be stressed" only serves to recall your stress. Be positive instead; "I want to be relaxed".

Would there be a negative consequence if I achieved what I wanted?

If there is a negative consequence to your goal, what would it be? If you spend more time with your family, will your work begin to suffer? Stop right here if you can see a difficulty, and resolve this issue as a separate problem.

When do I want it? What is the time frame? How will I know when I have succeeded? What am I going to see, hear or feel?

Consider each element of this stage carefully and you will learn just where you want to go. This makes the process more effective.

What steps must I take to achieve my goal?

Look at precisely what needs to be done to get where you want to be, plan it out in manageable stages and get going!

Resolve a few problems in this way and it will soon become second nature. No more time-wasting indecision about what to do. You'll know how to choose the course of action that best suits you and your particular needs.

TAP INTO
ENDLESS
CREATIVITY

Do you wonder where people get all their ideas from? Learn the following simple three-part strategy, which is equally applicable to working alone or in a team, and you'll never run out of ideas again. In the most creative meetings, one individual has all the ideas, another picks holes in them and a third person works out how to implement the good ones – they have taken on the roles of dreamer, critic and doer in the project – if you are working alone, you'll need to learn to find all three roles within yourself.

The DREAMER

Think of an instance when you were creative. Even the smallest hint of it will do. Remember how you felt then and imagine that you feel like that now. Position your body in a positive posture to reflect this. Now think about your goal. Perhaps you want to re-design the living room? Begin to generate concepts related to that. Let one flow from another. Don't censor any of your ideas at this stage as this will impinge on your creative flow. Make a list of them all.

The CRITIC

Now think back to an instance when you criticized an idea in a constructive manner. Adopt the feelings you had then and run through your list of ideas for redecorating the living room to see if any of them are feasible.

The DOER

Once you have one or two strong ideas, think of a time when you got things done. In the light of that experience, how would you implement these ideas. What needs to be in place?

This three-step process gives you the framework to come up with an idea that can be implemented without too many problems. To make it even more effective, imagine that the three roles are represented by three pairs of glasses. If you're working on your own, keep moving between the three roles freely, changing the glasses mentally, until you produce a completed plan of action.

MAKE BRAINSTORMING EFFORTLESS

Do you long for an efficient way of brainstorming that still makes sense to you in two days time? Try **Mind Maps** (originated by Tony Buzan), a great way to keep the benefits of writing lists and increase your creative efficiency at the same time. Producing a Mind Map encourages right and left brain activity. The process of creative thinking is more complicated than just writing a list – thoughts are far from linear – so don't make notes in sequence, instead associate your ideas with pictures and key words. It'll make them easier to recall in the long term as well.

Let your ideas flow and you'll make new links and associations between them.

Write your core topic in the centre of a page in capital letters. Allow your ideas to flow around the outside.

Write neatly and follow the line. Be precise and succinct in your wording.

Place your most important ideas close to the centre of the page.

Write without pausing. Use colour to enhance memory and incorporate doodles and sketches. You will find that ideas come pouring out. Show links between relevant items and consider the pros and cons of your plan. Above all, ENJOY THE PROCESS.

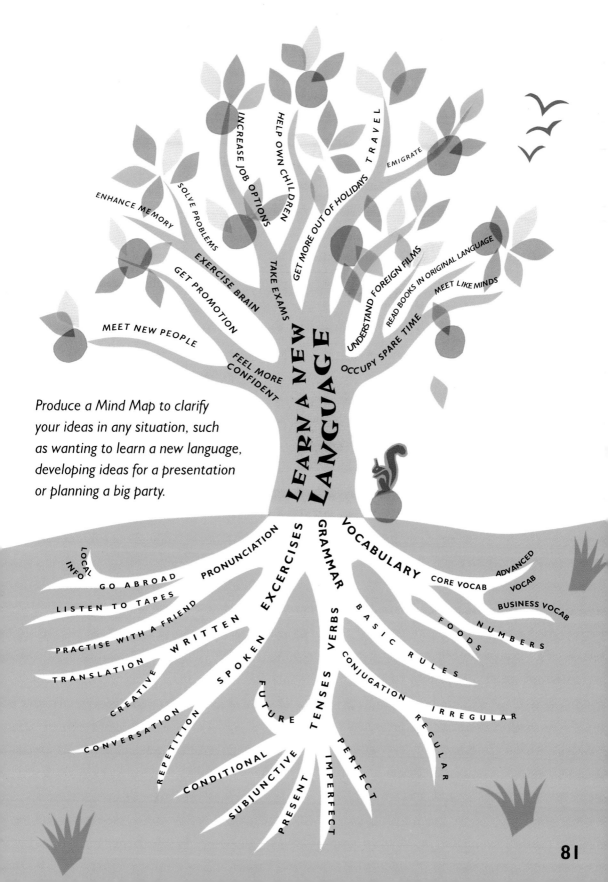

Produce a Mind Map to clarify
your ideas in any situation, such
as wanting to learn a new language,
developing ideas for a presentation
or planning a big party.

LEARN A NEW LANGUAGE

INCREASE JOB OPTIONS
HELP OWN CHILDREN
TRAVEL
EMIGRATE
SOLVE PROBLEMS
ENHANCE MEMORY
EXERCISE BRAIN
GET PROMOTION
TAKE EXAMS
GET MORE OUT OF HOLIDAYS
UNDERSTAND FOREIGN FILMS
READ BOOKS IN ORIGINAL LANGUAGE
MEET LIKE MINDS
MEET NEW PEOPLE
FEEL MORE CONFIDENT
OCCUPY SPARE TIME

LOCAL INFO
GO ABROAD
PRONUNCIATION
EXCERCISES
GRAMMAR
VOCABULARY
CORE VOCAB
ADVANCED VOCAB
BUSINESS VOCAB
LISTEN TO TAPES
PRACTISE WITH A FRIEND
WRITTEN
SPOKEN
VERBS
BASIC RULES
FOODS
NUMBERS
TRANSLATION
CREATIVE
CONVERSATION
REPETITION
FUTURE
TENSES
CONJUGATION
IRREGULAR
REGULAR
CONDITIONAL
SUBJUNCTIVE
PRESENT
IMPERFECT
PERFECT

LEARN TO ACCEPT CHANGE

Do you wander through life without knowing where you are going? Or do you have your life all mapped out, complete with action plan? Whichever way you live, think ahead to five years from now. What would you like achieve in those five years? Who would you like to be with? What do you want to learn? What about your financial situation?

Imagine that you are standing on a boat watching its wake stretch way out behind you. The wake represents the past as you will see it five years from now. In effect, you are looking back over the life that you are just embarking on. Everything you have achieved over those five years is clearly reflected in the water. What do you see?

Look down at the water and ask yourself what you need to do in order to be satisfied with your life in five years' time. Do you want to move or retrain for a new job? What do you have to do right now to achieve that? Where do you want to be at the end of the first year? And the second? And each year after? Do you need to make changes in your lifestyle to achieve this?

Visualize what you want to happen. Make the colours bright and the images large to jog your brain into recognizing the importance of your vision.

Plan your life carefully and you will soon see more opportunities appearing on the horizon. You'll be free to take advantage of them. Don't loose your flexibility, but steer your boat in the direction you want to go in and set the path for your future.

SHOOT
FOR THE
MOON

Have you ever settled for second-best because you didn't aim high enough? For example, have you accepted a small pay rise instead of putting faith in your abilities and pushing for more money? Or allowed a second-rate relationship to continue instead of trying to improve it?

Just like a pole-vaulter on the athletics field, you have to aim higher than the bar to clear it.

AIM FOR THE STARS TO JUMP OVER THE MOON

If you don't have goals in life, you may well end up with less than you deserve. By setting your expectations higher, you will achieve much more. If you aim to be the best as an artist, an athlete, a parent or in whatever you do, you will put more effort into succeeding than if you just had mediocre expectations of yourself.

You will gain the confidence to ask for more from life as you gradually increase your demands on yourself. Apply your new-found expectations to work and relationships and set high goals for achieving what you want in life.

By thinking positively and aiming high, you are putting a spring in your step to help you jump. Just like the cow who jumped over the moon!

SPELLING

IT RIGHT!

Do you find spelling problematic? Even if the answer to that is "No", it's worth reading on to find effective and enjoyable techniques to improve your spelling and make it an interesting process.

Some people try to spell phonetically, but that's not the best way. ("Phonetically" can't even be spelt phonetically!) Individuals who are good at spelling often use a visual image to help them along.

Imagine the letters of the word "Yellow" spelt out in front of you. Place them slightly up and to the left, which is where you tend to remember images. Make the image of the word very bright and clear. Visualize it in front of you and read the letters off to yourself.

N-E-C-E-S-S-A-R-Y

NEXT TRY A WORD THAT YOU STRUGGLE WITH. FOR EXAMPLE, "NECESSARY" CAUSES MANY PEOPLE PROBLEMS!

Visualize this word spelt out in front of you and look at the image that you see. Are there gaps where you're not sure of the spelling? Write down what you think is the correct spelling and then check it. The gaps in your visual image will start to fill as you correct your mistakes. Soon you will have the right spelling in your visual image; write this out on paper to reinforce the image.

Stretch your abilities by spelling out a word backwards – ensuring that you know it back to front.

Make this more fun – especially for children – by asking them to imagine the words written across the chest of a cartoon character or on a banner behind an airplane.

BECOME INSTANTLY ENTHUSIASTIC

Are there times when you feel that everything
is on top of you, but you still need to be productive?
Try a simple technique to govern and boost your
levels of enthusiasm. You can also do this for other
emotions, such as happiness and excitement.

*Rate your emotion on a scale of one to ten.
In this case, a rating of "1" shows that you are so
unenthusiastic about life that you are almost
asleep. A rating of "10", however, indicates that
you are a positive dynamo with enough energy
to spring-clean the world.*

FIRST *rate how you feel on your scale.*

THEN *make yourself a half-point less enthusiastic,
for example down from "5" to "4.5". This shows that
you CAN manipulate the scale.*

NEXT turn up your enthusiasm levels by pushing your rating up towards 10. Notch up a half-point at a time. Work out the changes you need to make to your **posture**, **inner voice** and **facial expressions** to support your new enthusiasm.

If ever your motivation starts to slip, simply run through this process to get yourself back on track. Apply this to your other emotions as well.

You're a step away from finding the motivation to get everything done ...

1 2 3 4 5 6 7 8 9 10

CONTINUAL GRADUAL IMPROVEMENT

How do you reach your full potential? It takes time, very much like producing a vintage wine or a mature cheese, for your confidence to grow and for you to be your most effective.

Maybe you have financial, work or health worries? If you use the tools in this book, you will start to notice improvements in all areas of your life. Decision-making will become easier and you will be able to ask for what YOU want. To motivate yourself further, keep a journal of your daily progress. Write in it once a day for at least five minutes to keep a check on your progress.

Treat your five-minute writing slot as a regular daily appointment. Discipline yourself to turn up, even if you only stay at your desk for a couple of minutes.

Ask yourself three questions each day when you're writing:

"What did I do well today?"

"What do I want to improve on?"

"What do I want to achieve?"

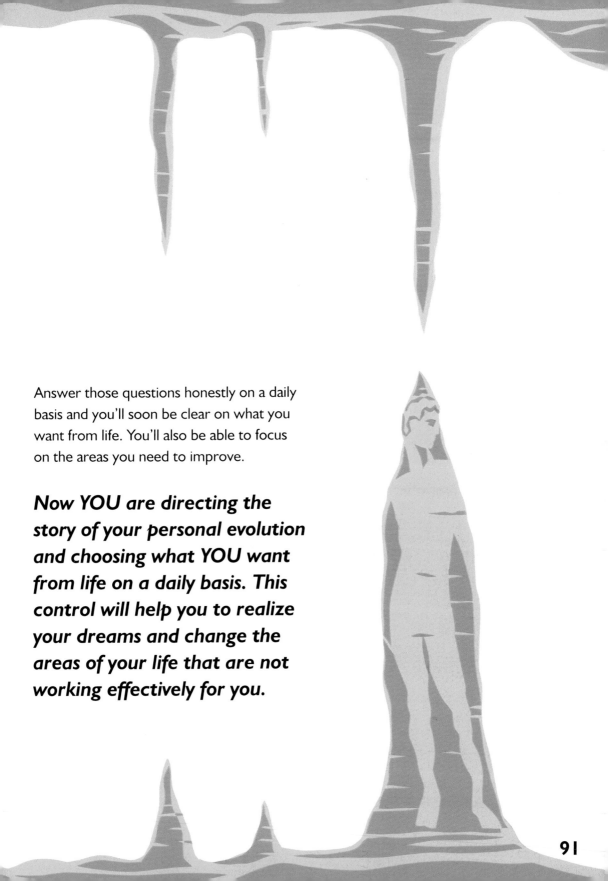

Answer those questions honestly on a daily basis and you'll soon be clear on what you want from life. You'll also be able to focus on the areas you need to improve.

Now YOU are directing the story of your personal evolution and choosing what YOU want from life on a daily basis. This control will help you to realize your dreams and change the areas of your life that are not working effectively for you.

PRACTICE MAKES PERFECT

Remember when you learned how to ride a bike? How many times did you tumble and how long was it before you felt confident? Perfecting any skill takes time and it is the process of practising that tells your brain to remember how to do it. Once your brain grasps this idea, like riding a bike, any new skill becomes easier and easier until it is second nature.

The four stages of learning are:

1 UNCONSCIOUS INCOMPETENCE

2 CONSCIOUS INCOMPETENCE

3 CONSCIOUS COMPETENCE

4 UNCONSCIOUS COMPETENCE

The four learning processes are:

> **1** *Not knowing that you do not know how to ride a bike – at this point you don't even know that you can learn to ride a bike.*

2 **Knowing that you do not know how to ride a bike – at this stage you fall off a lot.**

> **3** *Knowing that you know how to ride a bike – now you won't fall off as long as you focus all your attention on what you're doing.*

4 **You know how to ride a bike, but you are no longer conscious that you know – you don't even have to think about it to stay upright.**

The same goes for learning anything. Once you've moved out of that uncomfortable zone of wobbling about a fair bit, you're well on the way to having a new skill.

BE DECISIVE!

Do you find it hard to weigh options and commit to a decision? "On the one hand ... " and "On the other hand ... " are familiar phrases to us all. Internal conflicts like this waste your precious reserves of energy and stop you from getting things done.

Skiing is fast and fun ... invigorating ... time to free my mind ...

To resolve such conflict, for example when choosing a holiday destination, take your hands as a starting point.

Think **"On the one hand"**, look at your right hand and imagine the various benefits of **Plan A**.

Think **"On the other hand"**, and repeat the process with your left hand for **Plan B**.

Spend some time assessing each plan. Find the positive aspects in both. Then ask your unconscious if the plans are willing to integrate these aspects.

94

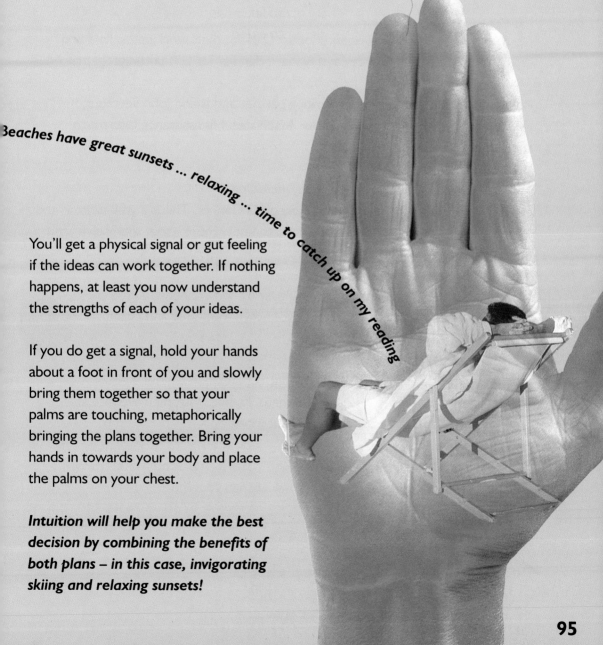

Beaches have great sunsets ... relaxing ... time to catch up on my reading

You'll get a physical signal or gut feeling if the ideas can work together. If nothing happens, at least you now understand the strengths of each of your ideas.

If you do get a signal, hold your hands about a foot in front of you and slowly bring them together so that your palms are touching, metaphorically bringing the plans together. Bring your hands in towards your body and place the palms on your chest.

Intuition will help you make the best decision by combining the benefits of both plans – in this case, invigorating skiing and relaxing sunsets!

WORDS FROM THE AUTHOR

Thank you to David Groves and Robert Dilts for their work in this field and especially to both John Grinder and Richard Bandler for first putting together NLP.

A personal thank you to mentor, writing partner and friend John Seymour, with whom I worked at John Seymour Associates. His assistance is so much appreciated.

There are many great books to read, including:
Introducing NLP by John Seymour and Joseph O'Connor. This is a well-written and comprehensive overview for anyone keen to know more about themselves and their interactions with others;

Awaken the Giant Within and *Unlimited Power* by Tony Robbins. These are inspirational books from the world's best-known motivator and coach.

Where to go next:
If you've enjoyed this taste of NLP, why not contact John Seymour Associates, providers of NLP courses from two hours to 20 days. Visit their website at **www.johnseymour-nlp.co.uk**, to find out more.

If you feel like a bite-size course online, visit me at **www.3courselunch.com**, where you will find video footage that may change your life ...